50 Oldest Sushi Styles in Japan Recipes

By: Kelly Johnson

Table of Contents

- Narezushi (Fermented Fish Sushi)
- Funazushi (Ancient Carp Sushi from Shiga)
- Funa Zushi (Salted and Fermented Goldfish Sushi)
- Haya Zushi (Early Fast-Fermented Sushi)
- Bo Zushi (Stick or Rod Sushi)
- Oshi Zushi (Pressed Sushi)
- Hako Zushi (Box Sushi from Osaka)
- Saba Zushi (Mackerel Pressed Sushi)
- Masu Zushi (Trout Sushi from Toyama)
- Iwakuni Zushi (Layered Box Sushi from Yamaguchi)
- Kakinoha Zushi (Persimmon Leaf Sushi from Nara)
- Hoba Zushi (Magnolia Leaf-Wrapped Sushi)
- Sasazushi (Bamboo Leaf Sushi from Nagano)
- Sugata Zushi (Whole Fish Sushi)
- Ayu Sugata Zushi (Sweetfish Whole-Body Sushi)
- Battera (Osaka-Style Pressed Mackerel Sushi)
- Edo-mae Sushi (Classic Tokyo Nigiri Style)
- Gunkan Maki (Battleship Roll)
- Temari Zushi (Handball-Shaped Sushi)
- Chirashi Zushi (Scattered Sushi)
- Tazuna Zushi (Striped Ribbon Sushi)
- Mushi Zushi (Steamed Sushi from Kansai)
- Warazuto Zushi (Rice-Stuffed Straw Sushi)
- Hokkaido Ika Meshi (Squid Sushi with Rice Filling)
- Tsuruga Zushi (Hand-Pressed Sushi from Fukui)
- Karei Zushi (Flounder Sushi from Shimane)
- Akagai Zushi (Ark Shell Sushi)
- Ko-Hada Zushi (Gizzard Shad Sushi)
- Tai Zushi (Sea Bream Sushi)
- Katsuo Zushi (Bonito Sushi)
- Ika Zushi (Squid Sushi)
- Anago Zushi (Saltwater Eel Sushi)
- Unagi Zushi (Freshwater Eel Sushi)
- Kohaku Namasu Zushi (Red-and-White Vinegared Sushi)
- Kasuzuke Zushi (Sake Lees-Marinated Sushi)

- Ebi Zushi (Shrimp Sushi)
- Maguro Zushi (Tuna Sushi)
- Kaki Zushi (Oyster Sushi)
- Yari Ika Zushi (Spear Squid Sushi)
- Ise Ebi Zushi (Spiny Lobster Sushi)
- Engawa Zushi (Fluke Fin Sushi)
- Shimesaba Zushi (Vinegared Mackerel Sushi)
- Kohada Bo Zushi (Whole Gizzard Shad Sushi)
- Kinmedai Zushi (Golden Eye Snapper Sushi)
- Nodoguro Zushi (Blackthroat Seaperch Sushi)
- Bafun Uni Zushi (Horse Urchin Sushi)
- Murasaki Uni Zushi (Purple Urchin Sushi)
- Tarako Zushi (Salted Cod Roe Sushi)
- Kazunoko Zushi (Herring Roe Sushi)
- Fugu Zushi (Blowfish Sushi)

Narezushi (Fermented Fish Sushi)

Ingredients

- 1 whole fish (mackerel, trout, or carp), gutted and cleaned
- 1/2 cup salt
- 2 cups cooked sushi rice

Instructions

1. Rub fish with salt and let ferment in an airtight container for 1–3 months.
2. Rinse the fish and pack it with sushi rice.
3. Ferment for another few days before serving sliced.

Funazushi (Ancient Carp Sushi from Shiga)

Ingredients

- 1 whole funa (crucian carp), gutted and cleaned
- 1/2 cup salt
- 2 cups cooked sushi rice

Instructions

1. Salt fish heavily and let ferment in an airtight container for 6 months.
2. Rinse, then pack fish with sushi rice and ferment for another few weeks.
3. Slice and serve with sake.

Funa Zushi (Salted and Fermented Goldfish Sushi)

Ingredients

- 1 small funa (goldfish carp), gutted and cleaned
- 1/2 cup salt
- 2 cups cooked sushi rice

Instructions

1. Salt fish and store in an airtight container for several months.
2. Rinse and press with sushi rice for additional fermentation.
3. Slice and serve.

Haya Zushi (Early Fast-Fermented Sushi)

Ingredients

- 2 cups cooked sushi rice
- 6 slices pickled fish (mackerel or salmon)
- 1 tbsp rice vinegar

Instructions

1. Lightly press rice into a mold.
2. Place pickled fish on top and press again.
3. Let sit for a few hours before slicing and serving.

Bo Zushi (Stick or Rod Sushi)

Ingredients

- 2 cups cooked sushi rice
- 6 slices mackerel or salmon
- 1 bamboo mat for rolling

Instructions

1. Place a sheet of plastic wrap on a bamboo mat.
2. Layer fish slices, then spread sushi rice on top.
3. Roll tightly into a log and press firmly.
4. Slice and serve.

Oshi Zushi (Pressed Sushi)

Ingredients

- 2 cups cooked sushi rice
- 6 slices cured mackerel or salmon
- 1 oshibako (wooden sushi mold)

Instructions

1. Press rice into the mold and layer fish on top.
2. Press firmly, then slice into rectangular pieces.
3. Serve with pickled ginger.

Hako Zushi (Box Sushi from Osaka)

Ingredients

- 2 cups cooked sushi rice
- 6 slices cooked eel or shrimp
- 1 wooden box mold

Instructions

1. Press sushi rice into the mold.
2. Add eel or shrimp, then press again.
3. Slice into bite-sized squares before serving.

Saba Zushi (Mackerel Pressed Sushi)

Ingredients

- 2 cups cooked sushi rice
- 6 slices cured mackerel
- 1 tbsp rice vinegar

Instructions

1. Place mackerel slices in a sushi mold.
2. Add rice on top and press firmly.
3. Slice and serve with pickled ginger.

Masu Zushi (Trout Sushi from Toyama)

Ingredients

- 2 cups cooked sushi rice
- 6 slices trout
- 6 bamboo leaves

Instructions

1. Line a mold with bamboo leaves.
2. Add sushi rice, then layer trout on top.
3. Press and let rest before slicing and serving.

Iwakuni Zushi (Layered Box Sushi from Yamaguchi)

Ingredients

- 2 cups cooked sushi rice
- 1/2 cup flaked cooked fish (mackerel or sea bream)
- 1/4 cup thinly sliced shiitake mushrooms
- 1/4 cup finely chopped egg omelet
- 1 tbsp rice vinegar
- 1 wooden sushi mold

Instructions

1. Layer sushi rice at the bottom of the mold.
2. Add layers of fish, mushrooms, and egg.
3. Press firmly, then slice and serve.

Kakinoha Zushi (Persimmon Leaf Sushi from Nara)

Ingredients

- 2 cups cooked sushi rice
- 6 slices cured mackerel or salmon
- 6 persimmon leaves

Instructions

1. Shape sushi rice into small rectangular pieces.
2. Top each with a slice of fish and wrap in a persimmon leaf.
3. Let rest for a few hours before serving.

Hoba Zushi (Magnolia Leaf-Wrapped Sushi)

Ingredients

- 2 cups cooked sushi rice
- 6 slices smoked trout or salted salmon
- 6 magnolia leaves

Instructions

1. Shape sushi rice into small rectangles.
2. Place fish slices on top and wrap each piece in a magnolia leaf.
3. Let sit for a few hours before serving.

Sasazushi (Bamboo Leaf Sushi from Nagano)

Ingredients

- 2 cups cooked sushi rice
- 6 slices pickled fish (salmon, mackerel)
- 6 bamboo leaves

Instructions

1. Shape rice into small rectangles and place fish slices on top.
2. Wrap each piece with a bamboo leaf and press gently.
3. Let sit for a few hours before serving.

Sugata Zushi (Whole Fish Sushi)

Ingredients

- 1 small whole fish (mackerel or horse mackerel), cleaned and deboned
- 2 cups cooked sushi rice
- 1 tbsp rice vinegar

Instructions

1. Marinate the fish in rice vinegar for 30 minutes.
2. Stuff the fish with sushi rice, pressing gently.
3. Slice and serve.

Ayu Sugata Zushi (Sweetfish Whole-Body Sushi)

Ingredients

- 1 whole ayu (sweetfish), cleaned and deboned
- 2 cups cooked sushi rice
- 1 tbsp rice vinegar

Instructions

1. Marinate the fish in rice vinegar for 30 minutes.
2. Stuff the fish with sushi rice, pressing gently.
3. Slice and serve.

Battera (Osaka-Style Pressed Mackerel Sushi)

Ingredients

- 2 cups cooked sushi rice
- 6 slices cured mackerel
- 1 oshibako (wooden sushi mold)

Instructions

1. Press rice into the mold and layer mackerel slices on top.
2. Press firmly, then slice into pieces.
3. Serve with pickled ginger.

Edo-mae Sushi (Classic Tokyo Nigiri Style)

Ingredients

- 2 cups cooked sushi rice
- 6 slices tuna, shrimp, or squid
- 1 tbsp wasabi
- 1 tbsp soy sauce

Instructions

1. Shape small mounds of rice with your hands.
2. Spread a small amount of wasabi on each fish slice.
3. Press fish onto the rice and serve with soy sauce.

Gunkan Maki (Battleship Roll)

Ingredients

- 2 cups cooked sushi rice
- 6 sheets nori (seaweed), cut into strips
- 6 tbsp salmon roe or uni (sea urchin)

Instructions

1. Shape sushi rice into small oval mounds.
2. Wrap nori around the rice, leaving space on top.
3. Fill the top with salmon roe or uni.

Temari Zushi (Handball-Shaped Sushi)

Ingredients

- 2 cups cooked sushi rice
- 6 slices salmon, tuna, or shrimp

Instructions

1. Place a slice of fish on plastic wrap, then add a small ball of rice.
2. Wrap tightly and shape into a round ball.
3. Unwrap and serve.

Chirashi Zushi (Scattered Sushi)

Ingredients

- 2 cups cooked sushi rice
- 1/2 cup sashimi-grade fish (tuna, salmon, shrimp), sliced
- 1/4 cup sliced cucumbers
- 1 tbsp ikura (salmon roe)
- 1 tbsp shredded nori
- 1 tsp pickled ginger

Instructions

1. Spread sushi rice in a bowl.
2. Arrange fish, cucumbers, and salmon roe on top.
3. Garnish with shredded nori and pickled ginger before serving.

Tazuna Zushi (Striped Ribbon Sushi)

Ingredients

- 2 cups cooked sushi rice
- 6 thin slices salmon, tuna, and egg omelet
- 1 sheet nori (seaweed)

Instructions

1. Arrange alternating strips of fish and omelet diagonally on plastic wrap.
2. Place a small mound of rice on top and wrap tightly.
3. Slice into bite-sized pieces and serve.

Mushi Zushi (Steamed Sushi from Kansai)

Ingredients

- 2 cups cooked sushi rice
- 1/2 cup unagi (grilled eel)
- 1/4 cup shiitake mushrooms, sliced
- 1 tbsp soy sauce
- 1 tbsp mirin
- 1 egg, beaten

Instructions

1. Mix soy sauce and mirin with mushrooms and simmer.
2. Layer sushi rice in a bowl, top with eel, mushrooms, and egg.
3. Steam for 5 minutes and serve warm.

Warazuto Zushi (Rice-Stuffed Straw Sushi)

Ingredients

- 2 cups cooked sushi rice
- 6 pieces pickled fish (mackerel or salmon)
- Straw wrapping (optional)

Instructions

1. Shape sushi rice into logs and wrap with fish.
2. Tie in straw bundles and let rest for 1 hour before serving.

Hokkaido Ika Meshi (Squid Sushi with Rice Filling)

Ingredients

- 2 small squid, cleaned
- 1 cup cooked sushi rice
- 2 tbsp soy sauce
- 1 tbsp mirin
- 1 tbsp sake

Instructions

1. Stuff squid with sushi rice and seal with toothpicks.
2. Simmer in soy sauce, mirin, and sake for 20 minutes.
3. Slice and serve.

Tsuruga Zushi (Hand-Pressed Sushi from Fukui)

Ingredients

- 2 cups cooked sushi rice
- 6 slices mackerel or white fish
- 1 tbsp rice vinegar

Instructions

1. Press rice into a mold and top with fish.
2. Press again and slice before serving.

Karei Zushi (Flounder Sushi from Shimane)

Ingredients

- 2 cups cooked sushi rice
- 6 slices flounder (lightly marinated in vinegar)

Instructions

1. Shape rice into small mounds.
2. Press a flounder slice on top and serve.

Akagai Zushi (Ark Shell Sushi)

Ingredients

- 2 cups cooked sushi rice
- 6 slices ark shell (akagai)

Instructions

1. Shape rice into small oval mounds.
2. Press an ark shell slice onto each mound and serve.

Ko-Hada Zushi (Gizzard Shad Sushi)

Ingredients

- 2 cups cooked sushi rice
- 6 slices ko-hada (gizzard shad, lightly cured)

Instructions

1. Shape rice into small mounds.
2. Place a ko-hada slice on each and serve.

Tai Zushi (Sea Bream Sushi)

Ingredients

- 2 cups cooked sushi rice
- 6 slices sea bream (tai)
- 1 tbsp rice vinegar

Instructions

1. Lightly brush sea bream slices with rice vinegar.
2. Shape sushi rice into small mounds.
3. Place a slice of sea bream on top, pressing gently.

Katsuo Zushi (Bonito Sushi)

Ingredients

- 2 cups cooked sushi rice
- 6 slices seared bonito (katsuo)
- 1 tbsp soy sauce
- 1 tsp grated ginger

Instructions

1. Lightly sear bonito slices and marinate in soy sauce for 10 minutes.
2. Shape sushi rice into small mounds.
3. Place bonito slices on top and serve with grated ginger.

Ika Zushi (Squid Sushi)

Ingredients

- 2 cups cooked sushi rice
- 6 slices fresh squid (ika)
- 1 tbsp soy sauce
- 1/2 tsp wasabi

Instructions

1. Shape sushi rice into small mounds.
2. Lightly brush squid slices with soy sauce.
3. Place squid slices on top, adding a small dab of wasabi underneath.

Anago Zushi (Saltwater Eel Sushi)

Ingredients

- 2 cups cooked sushi rice
- 1 fillet anago (saltwater eel)
- 1 tbsp soy sauce
- 1 tbsp mirin
- 1 tsp sugar

Instructions

1. Simmer anago in soy sauce, mirin, and sugar for 10 minutes.
2. Shape sushi rice into small mounds.
3. Place eel slices on top and brush with sauce.

Unagi Zushi (Freshwater Eel Sushi)

Ingredients

- 2 cups cooked sushi rice
- 1 fillet unagi (grilled freshwater eel)
- 1 tbsp eel sauce (unagi tare)
- 1/2 sheet nori (optional, for securing)

Instructions

1. Warm unagi in a pan and brush with eel sauce.
2. Shape sushi rice into small mounds.
3. Place unagi slices on top, securing with a thin strip of nori if desired.

Kohaku Namasu Zushi (Red-and-White Vinegared Sushi)

Ingredients

- 2 cups cooked sushi rice
- 1/2 cup thinly sliced daikon radish
- 1/2 cup thinly sliced carrot
- 2 tbsp rice vinegar
- 1 tbsp sugar
- 1/2 tsp salt

Instructions

1. Mix daikon and carrot with vinegar, sugar, and salt; let sit for 10 minutes.
2. Shape sushi rice into small mounds or spread in a bowl.
3. Top with the pickled vegetables and serve.

Kasuzuke Zushi (Sake Lees-Marinated Sushi)

Ingredients

- 2 cups cooked sushi rice
- 6 slices fish (salmon or mackerel)
- 1/2 cup sake lees
- 1 tbsp mirin
- 1 tbsp sugar

Instructions

1. Mix sake lees, mirin, and sugar into a paste.
2. Coat fish slices with the paste and let marinate for 1 day.
3. Wipe off excess, then place fish on shaped sushi rice mounds.

Ebi Zushi (Shrimp Sushi)

Ingredients

- 6 large shrimp (ebi), boiled and butterflied
- 2 cups cooked sushi rice
- 1 tbsp rice vinegar

Instructions

1. Boil shrimp for 2 minutes, then cool and butterfly.
2. Shape sushi rice into small mounds.
3. Place shrimp on top, pressing gently.

Maguro Zushi (Tuna Sushi)

Ingredients

- 2 cups cooked sushi rice
- 6 slices fresh tuna (maguro)
- 1/2 tsp wasabi

Instructions

1. Shape sushi rice into small mounds.
2. Spread a small dab of wasabi on each slice of tuna.
3. Press tuna onto the rice and serve.

Kaki Zushi (Oyster Sushi)

Ingredients

- 6 fresh oysters, shucked
- 2 cups cooked sushi rice
- 1 tbsp soy sauce
- 1 tbsp lemon juice
- 1/2 sheet nori, cut into thin strips

Instructions

1. Lightly sear or steam oysters for 1–2 minutes.
2. Drizzle with soy sauce and lemon juice.
3. Shape sushi rice into small mounds and place an oyster on top.
4. Secure with a thin strip of nori if needed.

Yari Ika Zushi (Spear Squid Sushi)

Ingredients

- 2 cups cooked sushi rice
- 6 thin slices spear squid (yari ika)
- 1/2 tsp wasabi
- 1 tbsp soy sauce

Instructions

1. Shape sushi rice into small mounds.
2. Spread a small dab of wasabi on each piece of squid.
3. Press squid onto the rice and lightly brush with soy sauce before serving.

Ise Ebi Zushi (Spiny Lobster Sushi)

Ingredients

- 6 pieces spiny lobster tail, cooked and sliced
- 2 cups cooked sushi rice
- 1 tbsp yuzu juice
- 1/2 tsp salt
- 1/2 sheet nori, cut into thin strips

Instructions

1. Toss lobster slices with yuzu juice and salt.
2. Shape sushi rice into small mounds.
3. Place lobster on top and secure with a thin strip of nori if desired.

Engawa Zushi (Fluke Fin Sushi)

Ingredients

- 6 slices fluke fin (engawa)
- 2 cups cooked sushi rice
- 1/2 tsp wasabi
- 1 tbsp ponzu sauce

Instructions

1. Shape sushi rice into small mounds.
2. Spread a small dab of wasabi on each slice of engawa.
3. Press engawa onto the rice and drizzle with ponzu sauce.

Shimesaba Zushi (Vinegared Mackerel Sushi)

Ingredients

- 2 cups cooked sushi rice
- 6 slices vinegar-marinated mackerel (shimesaba)
- 1 tbsp rice vinegar
- 1/2 tsp sugar

Instructions

1. Lightly marinate mackerel slices in vinegar and sugar for 10 minutes.
2. Shape sushi rice into small mounds.
3. Press mackerel slices onto the rice and serve.

Kohada Bo Zushi (Whole Gizzard Shad Sushi)

Ingredients

- 2 whole gizzard shad (kohada), filleted and lightly cured
- 2 cups cooked sushi rice
- 1 tbsp rice vinegar
- 1/2 tbsp sugar
- 1/2 tsp salt

Instructions

1. Marinate filleted kohada in a mixture of vinegar, sugar, and salt for 30 minutes.
2. Shape sushi rice into a long, rod-like form.
3. Lay the whole fillet over the rice and press gently.
4. Slice into bite-sized pieces before serving.

Kinmedai Zushi (Golden Eye Snapper Sushi)

Ingredients

- 6 slices kinmedai (golden eye snapper), lightly torched
- 2 cups cooked sushi rice
- 1/2 tsp wasabi
- 1 tbsp soy sauce

Instructions

1. Shape sushi rice into small mounds.
2. Place a small dab of wasabi on each slice of kinmedai.
3. Press the fish onto the rice and lightly brush with soy sauce.

Nodoguro Zushi (Blackthroat Seaperch Sushi)

Ingredients

- 6 slices nodoguro (blackthroat seaperch), lightly torched
- 2 cups cooked sushi rice
- 1 tbsp ponzu sauce
- 1/2 tsp grated daikon

Instructions

1. Shape sushi rice into small mounds.
2. Lightly torch the nodoguro slices.
3. Place fish on rice and top with ponzu sauce and grated daikon.

Bafun Uni Zushi (Horse Urchin Sushi)

Ingredients

- 6 pieces bafun uni (horse sea urchin)
- 2 cups cooked sushi rice
- 6 strips nori (seaweed)

Instructions

1. Shape sushi rice into small oval mounds.
2. Wrap each mound with a strip of nori, leaving space at the top.
3. Spoon uni onto the top and serve.

Murasaki Uni Zushi (Purple Urchin Sushi)

Ingredients

- 6 pieces murasaki uni (purple sea urchin)
- 2 cups cooked sushi rice
- 6 strips nori (seaweed)

Instructions

1. Shape sushi rice into small oval mounds.
2. Wrap each mound with a strip of nori, leaving space at the top.
3. Spoon uni onto the top and serve.

Tarako Zushi (Salted Cod Roe Sushi)

Ingredients

- 6 slices tarako (salted cod roe)
- 2 cups cooked sushi rice
- 6 strips nori (seaweed)

Instructions

1. Shape sushi rice into small oval mounds.
2. Wrap each mound with a strip of nori.
3. Place tarako on top and serve.

Kazunoko Zushi (Herring Roe Sushi)

Ingredients

- 6 pieces kazunoko (herring roe)
- 2 cups cooked sushi rice
- 6 strips nori (seaweed)
- 1 tbsp soy sauce

Instructions

1. Lightly marinate kazunoko in soy sauce for 10 minutes.
2. Shape sushi rice into small oval mounds.
3. Wrap each mound with a strip of nori and top with kazunoko.

Fugu Zushi (Blowfish Sushi)

Ingredients

- 6 slices fugu (blowfish), thinly sliced
- 2 cups cooked sushi rice
- 1 tbsp ponzu sauce
- 1/2 tsp grated daikon

Instructions

1. Shape sushi rice into small mounds.
2. Place fugu slices on top and press gently.
3. Drizzle with ponzu sauce and garnish with grated daikon before serving.

www.ingramcontent.com/pod-product-compliance
Lightning Source LLC
LaVergne TN
LVHW081342060526
838201LV00055B/2808